Egg Money

Egg Money

T. CLEAR

MoonPath Press

Poetry
ISBN 978-1-970256-09-3

Cover photo: "Henopause" by Peggy Barnett

Author photo: by Peggy Barnett

Book design by Tonya Namura using Garamond Premier Pro

MoonPath Press, an imprint of Concrete Wolf Poetry Series,
is dedicated to publishing the finest poets
living in the U.S. Pacific Northwest.

MoonPath Press
c/o Concrete Wolf
PO Box 2220
Newport, OR 97365-0163

MoonPathPress@gmail.com

https://MoonPathPress.com

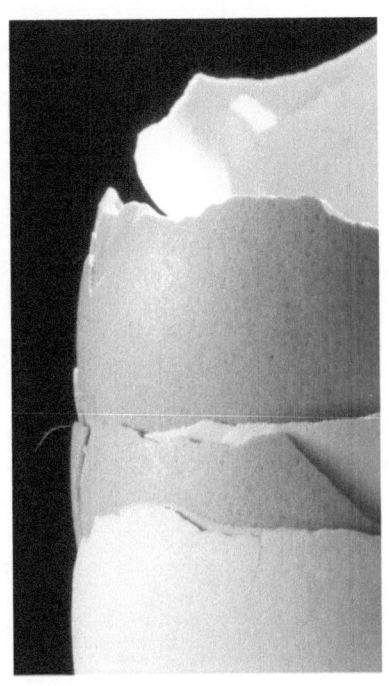

for my sons
Reilly Anderson, co-hen-wrangler
and
Nelson Anderson, coop builder

CONTENTS

Egg Money

PREAMBLE

Oh yes I fell in love, smitten
with ovum envy, with their high-cluck strut,
their busybody bicker over a spinach leaf.
Fell head over heels as they rose and fell
with the sun: up the planked ladder
as dusk descended, down again hungry
7–16 hours later. My clockwork beauties
plucking the bejesus out of their undowny coats.
Their winter-muddied flutter
and still: every egg a wonder
I thought would never end, never
become tiresome, death
by natural causes notwithstanding.

Until something slipped eellike,
owl-clever, swooped or slithered
where they fanned the feathered capes
of their wings, gathering warmth.
Ripped their heads to a limp gaze.
Gutted the gizzard, the pancreas,
the duodenal loop. A spilled slurry
laid hot and fly-flecked.
Just as quickly: the shovel, the pit,
the stamping-down, the dirt.
The last egg fried up in butter, the toast.

KEEPING FOWL

Not your grocery-store, boneless,
skinless thighs but blood-and-sinew
birds that fly nowhere, their footprint
diminished to a backyard run.

Edna, Fallopia, Billina: three hens
who pile into one nesting box
together, every morning.
A single feathered kerfuffle
of maternal clucks and coos.

Let out into the yard,
they make a dust spa
where they dig and roll
to smother mites.
I build a fence, a gate.
String netting overhead;
even so they stop dead-still
when an eagle passes over.

Summer evenings it's the girls
and me and a glass of wine,
awaiting the moment
when they wander back to the coop,
a single-file climb to the roost.
When you desire the daily egg locally laid
plus roasted hen for supper

you learn to draw a line in the straw.
When asked in airport security
if I have pets, I answer: yes,
two cats, three chickens.

LIVING IN THE HENHOUSE

There ain't nobody here but us chickens
—Louis Jordan

It's cozy here,
all this fluff afloat,

heaps of straw underfoot.
Housekeeping's a snap

with a feather duster.
Dang chickens

peck at our toenails
but there's the egg

money. Buys a trinket
or two for the wife.

She's partial to pink
hair combs and curlers.

I fancy the occasional
sour mash, a nip

before a snore.
Truth is, we do brood

now and again—
it's so tiny a hut.

We try not to get
our hackles up.

Feeling coopish,
we take a strut out in the yard

round about dawn,
sing our little hearts out.

Scratching out a life here
and it ain't half bad.

EGG MONEY

I count these days in multiples:
three chickens, three eggs, three dollars
for each half dozen sold to a neighbor

and plenty to spare for my own plate.
There was a time I stashed away
macaroni, canned tuna, kidney beans,

quarts of plums gleaned
from fence-leaning trees.
The basement cupboard

never quite full, a winter
of never enough work
pressing towards me

as the light thinned.
I scraped the pot until it squeaked,
tied the shoestring's last thread.

My mother taught me
how to conjure a meal
when none seemed possible.

How the last cup of flour,
last few dabs of butter
made enough biscuits

to quiet clamoring children.
But I needed chickens then.
Needed three dollars

in the middle of January.
Needed eggs, fried,
sunny-side up.

HEN FRENZY

After a few handfuls of fresh straw,
you'd think I'd recarpeted the coop
the way the five of them crowd in,
walk around and around inside,
bumping wings, lifting each foot high
before stepping down on the dry grass,
murmuring their soft hen murmurs
as if it were time to lay an egg.
Keeps them happy all day,
sixteen square feet such a novelty
you'd think they don't recall
it happens every few weeks.
They're easy that way—
a pile of weeds pulled from the garden,
vegetable-bin scraps, the odd lettuce
days past its last salad tossed
in a heap over the fence. They sprint,
heads down, a chicken free-for-all
that makes me think of the Altar Society
rummage sale my mom ran
once a year at St. Anthony's,
the way women crowded the doors
promptly at 9 a.m. to amass bargains
in Market Basket bags:
bleached-out infant undershirts
or woolen winter coats
with a few good years left,
as many as filled a paper sack, 99¢.

ON NOT GETTING EATEN BY A RACCOON

The one time I forgot to count the hens
before latching them in for the night,
of course I left one loose. You'd think
it wouldn't be so hard with only three.

I don't know where she roosted those long hours
separated from her sister-hens, no feather-heat
but her own. Somewhere lucky, absent
a beast out for a midnight snack.

In the morning I found her
egg-heavy, tapping the back door
with her beak, scolding
like a child I'd not sung to sleep.

If only she knew how often I've dreamed
I've left all three perched in the apple tree
with no more shelter than a canopy of clouds.
If she did, she might count her blessings.

But she's only a chicken, and chickens don't count.
I hope I do, tonight, and every night.
It might be the one thing
that keeps any of us alive.

FLYPAPER IN THE COOP

All it ever caught
was a clump of my hair
when I brushed too close
scraping the daily dung—
that and a few scattered gnats.
The ones I was after,
those big buggers
that swarmed every morning?
They wangled clear
of the spiraling tape.
If I was a fly,
I'd've starved to death
by now, suspended
with a lank of hair
above three hens,
a potholed run.
But why do I want
all those flies dead,
considering not everything
they do is grim?
For instance:
nothing breaks down
a turd pile faster
than maggots who gorge
on the very matter
that swaddled their gestation.
Did you know that a fly
can identify sugar
just by stepping on it?

And what I'd do
for their sticky pads
on each foot—
the walls I'd walk!
All too much to know.
But there's that yellow strip
hanging like a dead tongue
that announces what the end
of the world will sound like:
a lot of buzzing and whirring,
and not even one of these
carefully chosen words.

DOGMA

They covet the odd worm,
are smarter than they let on.

Egg production is limited
to roughly 600 per hen,

give or take an ovum or three.
Mud-puddle water tastes better

than fresh. If left to roam,
they'll return at dusk to perch

for the night, safe in the coop.
Sometimes all happiness requires

is a handful of dandelion greens
tossed into the run.

THE TWO EDNAS

With her white-as-privilege feathers
Edna-the-leghorn-hen gets up in the nest
and scratches away every last shred of straw
until she can drop that equally white ovum
onto a bare plywood bed. Thud.
Not a gram of chickenly regard.
No worry she'll suddenly go broody
in hopes of her own little buttercup-of-a-hatchling.
No siree, Bob—all merely perfunctory,
once every 23 hours.

One could say she's the spitting image
of Edna P. Couch, the white-wigged battle-axe
with lipstick blazing red as Edna-the-hen's
floppity comb. But that might be disrespectful
to my granny-in-law—have mercy!
—her name chiseled onto a gravestone
between two dead husbands
in Mt. Hermon, Louisiana. From whence
her barely sixteen-year-old daughter fled
to Seattle, as far from Mt. Hermon as possible

without tipping into the sea. Edna P. Couch
scowled with a face that could fry eggs
because a "Negro" played Dixieland jazz
when her grandson married me, and champagne
flowed like the Mississippi in a hurricane.
Her recounting for the local society page—
after the wedding, a nice ham supper was enjoyed

at the home of the groom's parents—was fiction
served up by the platterful, whitewashed down
with imaginary pitchers of fresh lemonade.

(I recall whiskey bottles, ashtrays,
Edna planted in the corner like a potted frown.)
Edna-the-leghorn-hen wears her inheritance
like a laurel, all pluck-and-bother
as she pecks the Rhode Island reds
down to their pin feathers. Molting,
she trails a fluttered wake. One might believe
angel plumage had rained down from heaven
if not for Edna P. Couch's legacy, God help me.
No place in this coop for her kind of hate.

EDNA GETS A FOOT MASSAGE

It isn't for pleasure
when I position her foot-side up
in my lap, post-pursuit & capture,
cooing sweet nothings to calm her kerfuffle.

Tucked snug beneath my arm,
I can feel her feathered heart tick
as I rub oil to smother mites
that'd ravage her feet, left unchecked.

No bigger than a fingertip,
the tiny meat-nub anchoring her toes
eases to my gentle pressure.
Edna droops her eyelids half-mast,

a moment so brief one might miss it
fixated on an upside-down bird
who by now has had enough,
wants back to the gravel-scratch run.

Edna flaps away—all flurry, all complaints—
pleasure so fleeting already it's taken wing.
I think, this must not be
what people mean when they say,

Don't miss the must-have chicken feet at Dim Sum House!

ON OVERHEARING THE HENS DISCUSS
HOW HUMANS ARE JUST LIKE THEM

(translated from Chicken)

You've seen how she fluffs
the nest every day,
brings in fresh straw?
Mark my clucks, before long
she'll carry it in her beak
instead of her claws.
Preens, too, I've seen her
through the window fussing
with her feathers.

Listen to her bukbuks
and buh*gawwwwks*—
I think she's trying to talk to us.
So adorable!

I've even seen her scratch for bugs
with a strange long-handled tool.
OMG.
Why doesn't she use her toes?

Eats corn, right off the cob.
Perches up on her balcony
at dusk: she *is* like us!

What do you wanna bet
one of these mornings
she'll trot out an entire brood
of golden-fluffed babies.
Lord knows she's stolen
every damn one of our eggs
and I *know* it doesn't take
this long to hatch a chick.

MAYDAY

6 a.m., and the chickens are yelling
a saw-edged measure of unneighborly noise.
Give it a few minutes

before I trip from my quilted haze
to see what's caused
all holy hell to break out.

Find nothing.
Is this their dawn chorus?
Do chickens sing?

I've seen them stop cluck-still
under a circling hawk
until danger's swooped from sight.

Watch them scramble without a squawk
to avoid a pink beribboned balloon
let loose from a party.

But this yelling—clearly not alarm
except maybe it's time for a fist
of beetle-bitten chard from the garden,

useless for my plate, perfect
for fowl-pecks. I'll get it back
tomorrow, transubstantiated

to a biscuit-brown egg. I believe
all things holy begin in forgiveness.

BIRDS OF A FEATHER

We're too old now to pillow-down
in shared bunks, my sisters and I,
but the daily bickers and clucks
persist as if we were six hens
roosted for the night wing to wing.
Even this can be a kind of love,
if you care enough to keep it up
as long as we have, seven decades
and counting. Harmony isn't everything.

Though the harmony we sang
elbow to elbow at the piano,
the "Hallelujah Chorus,"
or "For the Beauty of the Earth,"
was everything, especially
the wonder of our perfect pitch.
That we crowded together on the sofa
was also everything, always
room for one more, impossibly
squeezed hip to hip, laughing
as if there were no end
to this complicated affinity, no grief.

When we wandered from each other
and chose new sisters, honorary sisters,
who filled the gap when the squabbling
turned beak-sharp, claw-scratched,
we came back, eventually,

because time dulls the razor's
slash, the slap-quick words.
We came back and were glad for it.

My sisters are the buffer
between the world and me
even as our numbers have dwindled
from six to five, then four,
and another from Alzheimer's ravage.
They are my no-fault insurance policy
paid in full at birth, soon to expire.

RODENTS

We sought a warmer home
where no rain dripped, no spiders nested.

Began to scrape and claw a way in,
a little more each night, inch by inch

until a barricade appeared, nailed flush
to block our months of labor.

The sharpest tooth useless.
Bolted out, barbed out, left

to huddle as we've always huddled,
tunneled hungry underground.

We wait until dusk to venture out,
let our young run and tussle, ever watchful.

Lucky for a husk of half-chewed melon,
sometimes a peanut, a cabbage. Never picky.

Every night a trick to tempt us—
bait only the eldest can resist.

Last month we lost fifteen to the killing snap,
tender bodies chucked into a sack, tossed for trash.

They desire our eradication.
We'll outsmart their hate.
We'll never give up.

THE RAT CONSIDERS PETS

Some they coddle, like the slinky
beasts who stalk us every night,
who pass their days indoors
where they curl their animal
warmth into blanketed nests.

Others are barred from the Big House,
interned in a tiny hut with a ramp and perch,
sloppy eaters with curious pointed snouts
who fling the feed we're happy
to tidy up once they've roosted.

Some descend from the sky
to consume their fill from a tube
spilling with seeds. We empty it
every night in secret, each morning
the feast replenished.

Lucky, none they call *pup* on our parcel,
but sometimes we see one in the alley
let out on a leash, cuspids hidden under lip-flaps.
One breed named for its slaying skills.
Will we never be treasured?

Elders share tales of an oddly pigmented cousin
caged inside the Big House, whose belly grew
fat as a ten-pound sack of corn. Lived well
past a year, but few believe a rat can last
that long, running a wheel, going nowhere.

COOP REPAIRS

Mud underfoot like a rat
too many days dead in the alley.
The hens hold their feathers close
to the skin, not an inch of dry ground
and this rain, without mercy.

Plastic sheeting stapled against chicken wire
makes a quick job of keeping the wet out
before the wind lashes me sideways,
my parka useless in the torrent.
An armload of fresh straw and I'm done.

Not a bad place to sleep, I think,
nested snug in a shipping-pallet hut,
elbowed-in with chickens. No one will notice
my wings, withered where they once sprouted,
folded carefully out of sight.

EGRESS / INGRESS

The hens pace the run
like convicts, muttering
over mud and a month of rain.
Every day offers a new way out:
busted fence, torn wire,

gate half an inch slack.
They'll pillage my garden
for the love of a worm,
strip the lemon balm to twigs
in a midday breakout.

Should I remind them it's me
who keeps them from raccoons
who'd pull a bird's head
through chicken wire, given the chance?
That it's me who secures their shingled hut

each night before sleep?
Sometimes I dream of birds
not getting out but getting in,
a confetti'd flock, a brooder's dozen
of a species yet unknown

that joins my dozing girls
in a kaleidoscope of feathers
so dazzling it burns the eyes
of the coyotes pacing
the perimeter for fresh meat.

CHICKEN VIGIL

Who will believe me when I say
my hens forgo their daily dig for bugs
and choose instead to sit like saffron Buddhas
beside their sister-hen whose legs have failed,
whose wings lie limp as silk?

She won't eat until I push the bowl up close
and all three peck the mash as one.
Her wattle shrivels;
not an egg in months.
Her morning squawk's gone silent.

I've been accused of anthropomorphism
more than once, have seen a cat smile.
But maybe we have it backwards—
that it was a bird who first sat watch beside the dying,
and we were too busy evolving to notice.

MAY PARADISE KILLED MY CHICKEN

(Which sounds worse than it was,
but how else to get a perfect name like that
into a poem about a chicken losing its head?)

May Paradise took an ax, gave my chicken forty—

No. That's not it.
This was quick, on a stump,
with no lingering feathered steps.

I may never eat another chicken
after weeks of nursing a sick hen
on steel-cut oats and buttermilk.

Bedeviled by options, I waited too long:
cervical dislocation or asphyxiation?
Build a mini-gallows?

When she stopped drinking
and her wings hung sad like wrung-out rags,
thank God for friends who wield an ax.

Paradise killed with just one whack.

LAST SUPPER ON A BURNING PLANET

If this is the end of life as we know it, I'm going
to pick a fistful of parsley. Tomatoes too,
a quart of ripe Super Sweets. And beans,
tender green suspended in smoky light.
The sun, particle-obscured,
is a Halloween pumpkin
with no need of a menacing leer—
we're all scared as fuck
no matter how you slice it.

Out back in the chicken coop,
flies practice decomposition,
though maybe *practice* is the wrong word.
After millions of years they're pros
at what they do, light-years ahead of sad us.
So eat up, drink a toast to our ultimate demise,
because it's staring us down from an ashen sky
looking like a fly's eye, like thousands of ommatidia,
each one focused exactly on you.

REASONS TO CONTINUE

This one egg
bedded in straw,

golden-rose
in the middle of winter.

These three hens
fluffing the nest.

This blanket of moss
after summer's scorch.

These bare apple branches.
This cracked-shell moon

rising above mountains at dusk.

ACKNOWLEDGMENTS & GRATITUDE

The author would like to express gratitude to *Pine Row Press*, where the poem "Coop Repairs" first appeared.

OODLES OF THANKS TO:

The ever-present EasySpeak Seattle gang, whose ongoing presence ensures a generous reception to whatever I share at our twice-monthly open mic, and who has heard me cluck through every one of these poems.

Special thanks to Peggy Barnett and Mary Crane for affecting a chicken accent and taking part in the live reading of "Upon Overhearing the Hens Discuss How Humans Are Just Like Them."

The hens that came and went over my five-year fowl adventure: Betty, Billina, Coriander, Fallopia, Nutmeg, and Edna P. Couch, whose daily production of one precious egg each morning was met with awe, praise, and respect. They led me into a new universe where I passed many a balmy summer evening sitting on my deck, glass of chilled sauvignon blanc in hand, waiting for that moment when they headed up the henhouse ramp to roost for the night.

Lastly, warm thanks to Lana Hechtman Ayers, Managing Editor, Thomas A. Thomas, Assistant Managing Editor, and Tonya Namura, Book Designer for making the publication process a breeze.

ABOUT THE AUTHOR

Over her lifetime, Seattle poet T. Clear has always wanted more pets than only cats, dogs, hamsters, gerbils, and goldfish. In 2017 she made the decision to become a backyard chicken wrangler when she acquired three hens; and over the course of the next five years, added three more to her flock. This chicken obsession ended with their untimely demise in 2022 by an unidentified predator.

Over the past 50 years, her work has appeared in many publications, including *The American Journal of Poetry*, *Anti-Heroin Chic*, *Atlanta Review*, *Bayou*, *Bellingham Review*, *Cirque Journal*, *Common Ground Review*, *Crab Creek Review*, *Crannóg*, *Dunes Review*, *In Parentheses*, *Iron Horse Literary Review*, *Lily Poetry*, *The Mayo News*, *The Moth*, *Poetry Northwest*, *Raven Chronicles*, *Red Earth Review*, *The Rise Up Review*, *Scoundrel Time*, Seattle Metro's Art and Poetry on Buses Project, *Seattle Review*, *Sheila-Na-Gig Online*, *South Florida Poetry Journal*, *Tab Journal*, *Terrain.org*, *Thimble*

Literary Magazine, UCity Review, The Wax Paper, and *What Rough Beast*.

She's a founder of Floating Bridge Press and currently is an associate editor for *Bracken Magazine*. Her full-length book, *A House, Undone*, winner of the 2020 Sally Albiso Award, is available from MoonPath Press. Visit her online at TClearPoet.com.

www.ingramcontent.com/pod-product-compliance
Lightning Source LLC
Chambersburg PA
CBHW031706150626
46549CB00017B/3135